The Art of Piano Performance: Pedaling

By Professor Peter Coraggio   Illustrated by Jon J. Murakami

FEATURING...

MAESTRO PROFONDO
Musician extraordinaire

MUSABELLA
Profondo's lovely teaching assisstant

AGITATO
Neophyte student

Hmmm... Now where to begin?..

Oh yes... This is a piano...

...Unique among musical instruments.

Distinguished for its ability to create singing melodies and beautiful harmonic sonorities...

...yet at its heart the piano is essentially only a percussive device.

Most musical instruments are held when played and act as extensions of your body and voice. Musical tones are most often made by blowing or bowing.

The piano is not held when played, The pianist, flipping down levers (keys) with fingers, tosses hammers at strings, forcing them to vibrate and make tones.

KIDS! DO NOT DO THIS AT HOME!!!

© 1997 Neil A. Kjos Music Company, 4380 Jutland Drive, San Diego, California, 92117   GP412

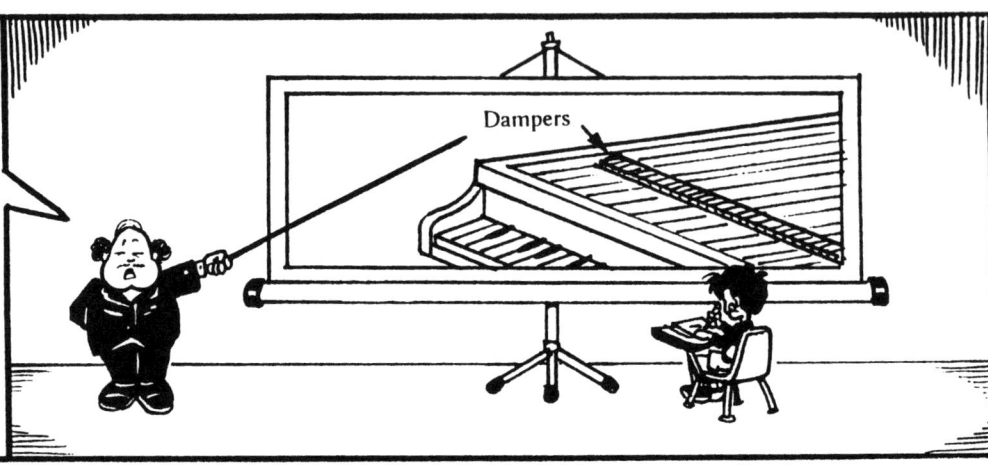
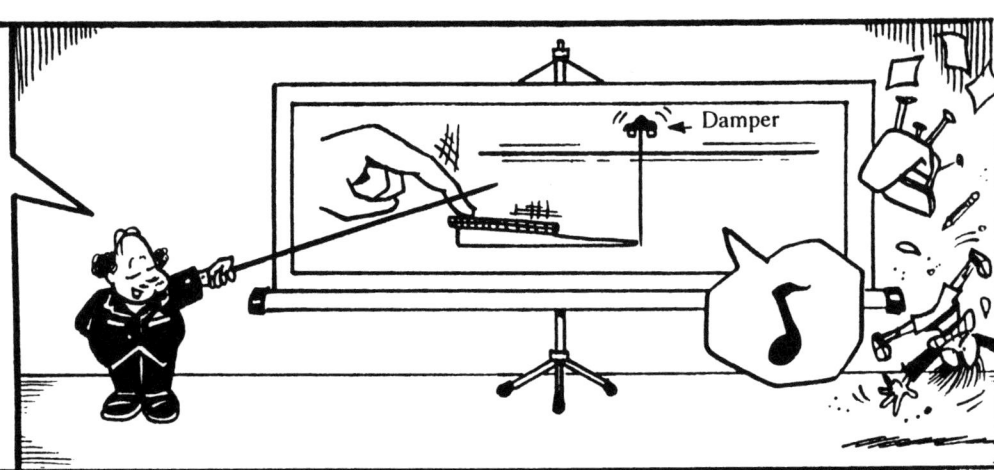
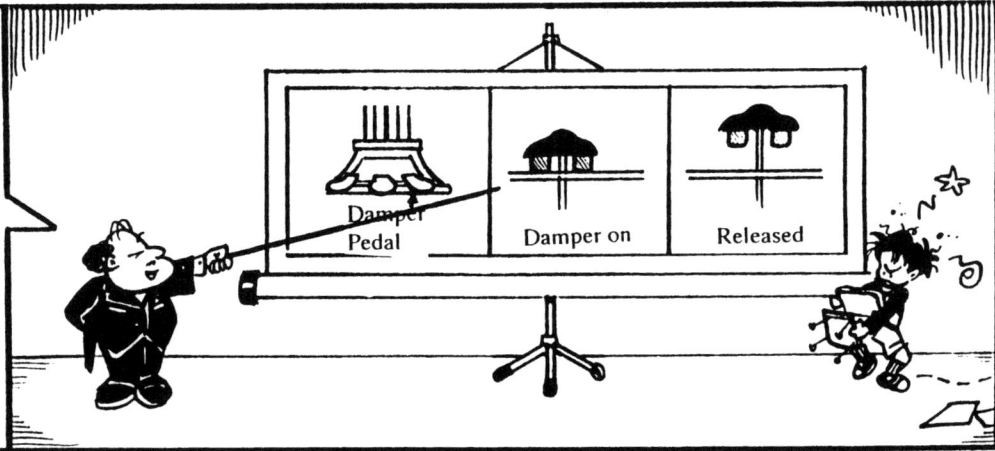
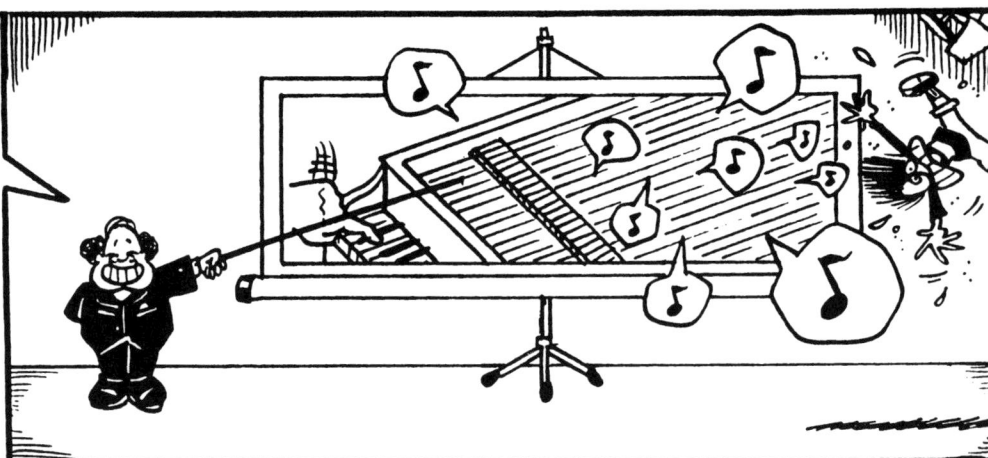

Begin by slowly lowering the damper pedal with your right foot until you feel some resistance. This is the pedal's "threshold" - the point at which the dampers begin to be lifted away from the strings.

The pedal threshold is the point of sensitive control. When the pedal is alternately gently depressed and released back to the threshold, a very soft rubbing sound like breathing may be heard from within the piano.

If the pedal is pushed down too far, the dampers will lift unnecessarily high off the strings and will thump strongly against the strings when the pedal is released.

The damper pedal may be compared to a light switch.

Lights are controlled by either on-off switches...

...or by dimmers which give continuous control from no light to full light.

Sensitive pianists treat the pedal similar to a light dimmer instead of an on-off switch. This allows a wide range of control from no pedal to full pedal.

How much gas pedal or brake pedal do you use while driving your car? This is an absurd question. How you use the pedals is determined by how fast you want the car to move or stop.

The pedals are controlled by your sense of momentum and your desire to go faster or slower. Usually you are not aware of your foot movement.

SYNCOPATED PEDAL is usually the first pedaling technique students learn. The pedal is depressed <u>after</u> the note or chord is played.

Syncopated Pedal

A good way to learn syncopated pedaling is to first close your eyes with your foot on the damper pedal at the pedal's threshold.

As another pianist plays various chords, gently lift and depress the pedal immediately upon hearing each new harmony.

You will quickly realize that <u>what controls the pedal is not the foot, but the ear!</u>

When you depress the pedal immediately after a note or chord is played, all of the piano's strings are instantly freed to vibrate. This helps create a beautiful singing tone and a rich piano sonority.

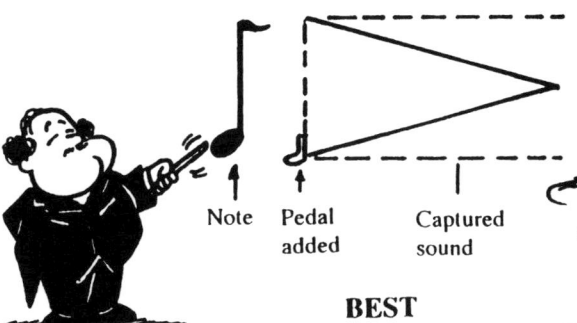

BEST TONE!!

If you depress the pedal too late, much of the fast fading sound is lost before being captured.

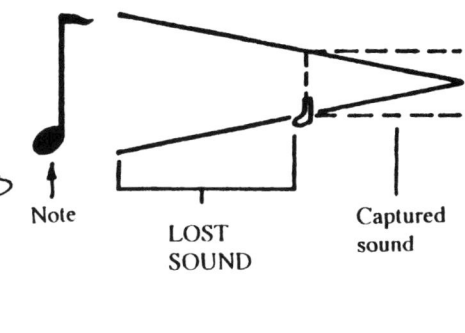

The Art of Piano Performance: Pedaling

By Professor Peter Coraggio   **Illustrated by Jon J. Murakami**

FEATURING...

MAESTRO PROFONDO — Musician extraordinaire

MUSABELLA — Profondo's lovely teaching assisstant

AGITATO — Neophyte student

In the first chapter, Master Profondo introduced the **Damper Pedal**.

The Damper Pedal is the pedal that controls the sound stoppers.

This is the keyboard artist's most important pedal.

He showed how to lower your foot to the pedal's **threshold** (the spot where the dampers begin to lift off the strings).

He also showed the pianist's basic pedal changing technique - **Syncopated Pedal** (the pedal is pressed down right after the note is played).

Chopin's *Marzuka in A Minor, Op. 17, No.4*

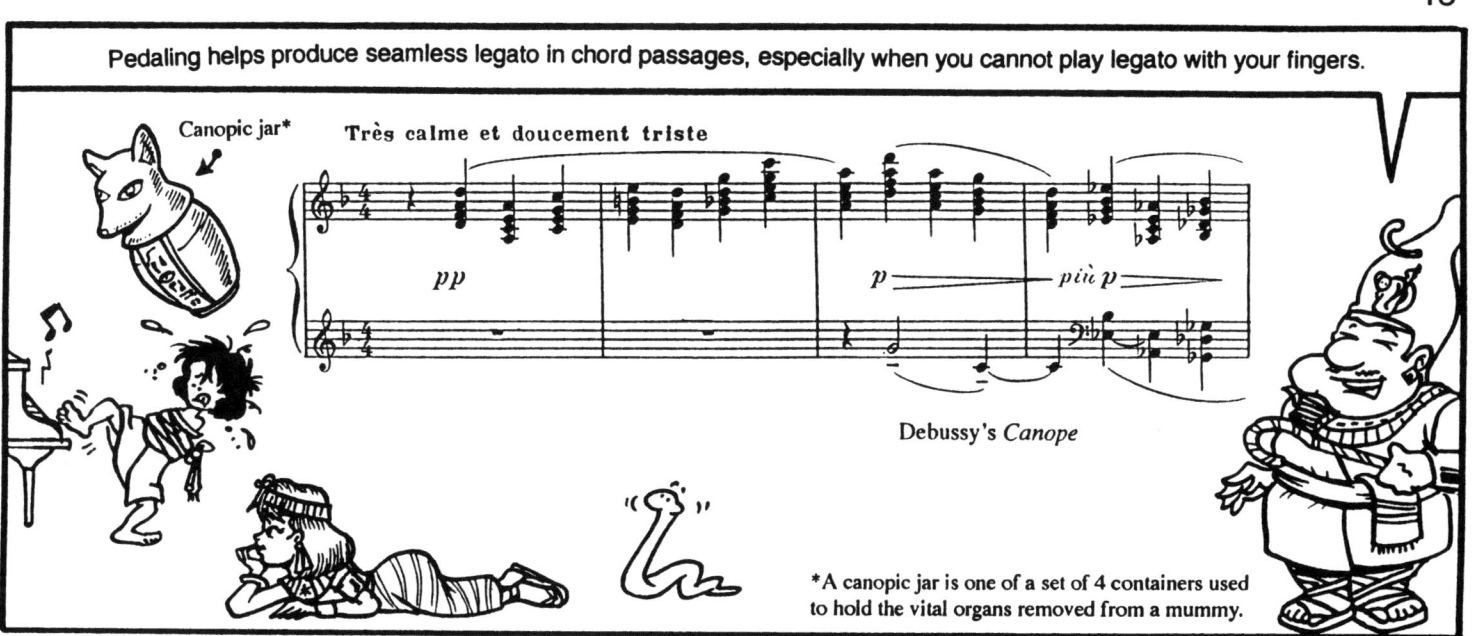

HALF-DAMPING

Don't you enjoy singing in the shower? The echoes of your voice make the sound more beautiful and you feel as if you are a star singing in front of a very large audience.

You know how much fun it is when you sing karaoke with lots of echo or hear someone play guitar through an amplifier with lots of echo.

The piano's sound can also be enhanced if you use the damper pedal in a special way.

EVERYONE'S A CRITIC OOOO...

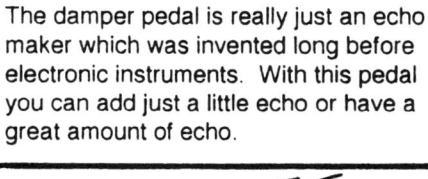

The damper pedal is really just an echo maker which was invented long before electronic instruments. With this pedal you can add just a little echo or have a great amount of echo.

Hey, Frederic!!! I think I'm on to something!!!

How do you do it?...

The right pedal is the controller of the sound stoppers (the dampers).

Squeeze the pedal down slowly until you feel a change of pressure under your right foot.

By careful testing and listening you can discover the point where the dampers start to come off the strings and echo begins to be heard as you play.

If you do this on an open grand piano you can see the dampers move gently off the strings.

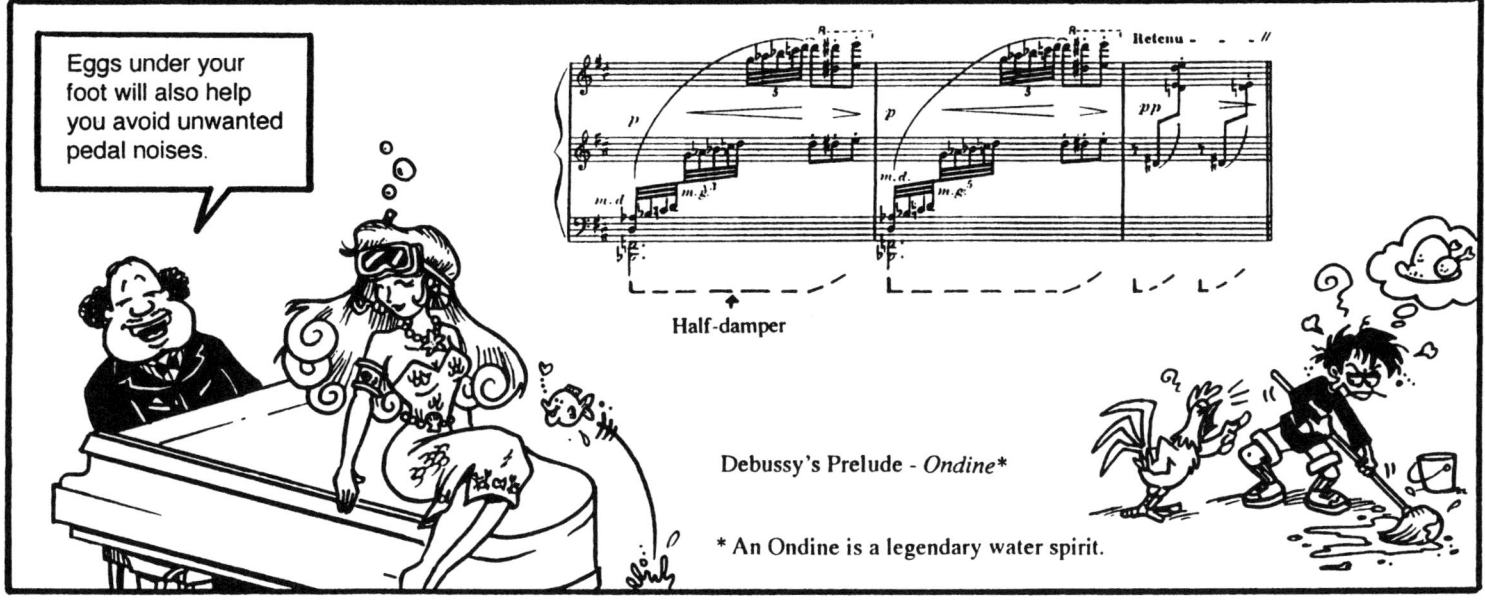

HALF PEDALING

Half-pedaling technique allows you to **erase unwanted extra sound** by briefly tapping or touching the dampers to the strings. This works best when you don't start with the dampers too far away from the strings.

1. Push the pedal down just far enough to take the dampers off the strings, enabling the strings to vibrate freely.

2. Gradually lift your foot, lowering the dampers until they lightly touch the strings.

3. Immediately push the pedal down once again to capture the amount of leftover sound that you want to keep.

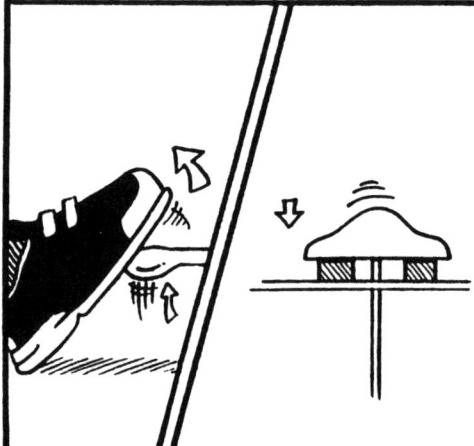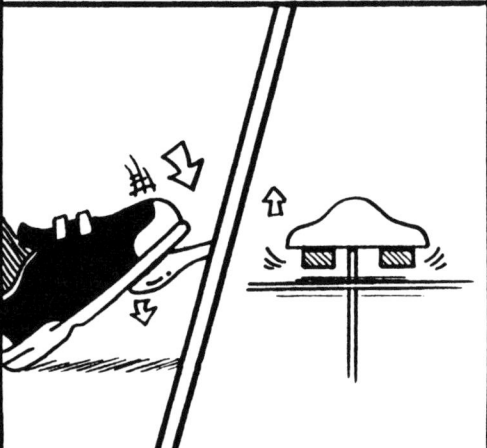

Half-pedaling requires sensitive control and continuous listening.

By letting the dampers gently touch the strings you can clear some of the sound of the short high strings while sustaining the sound of the long low strings.

Chopin's *Prelude in D-Flat Major*

Chopin, the absolute master of piano sound, always reminded his students to place the foot at the pedal's threshold for sensitive control of the sound.

Half-damping and **half-pedaling** are related. With half-damping, the dampers are always gently touching the strings. With half-pedaling, you let the dampers just touch the strings and then take them away again, letting them to continue vibrating at a lower level.

You can use half-damper and half-pedal techniques on any music played on the piano. Advanced pianists even use the pedal on music from the time of Bach.

J.S. Bach's *Prelude in E-Flat Minor, WTC 1*

Half-damping and half-pedaling techniques are used in some sections of almost all 19th century Romantic and 20th century music.

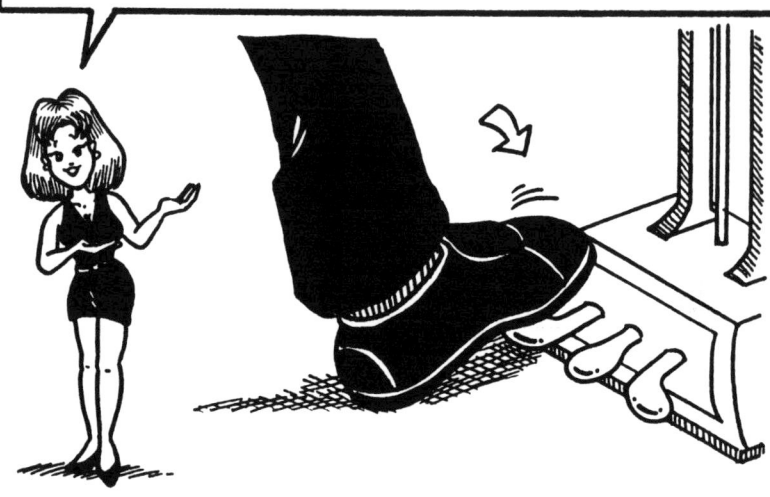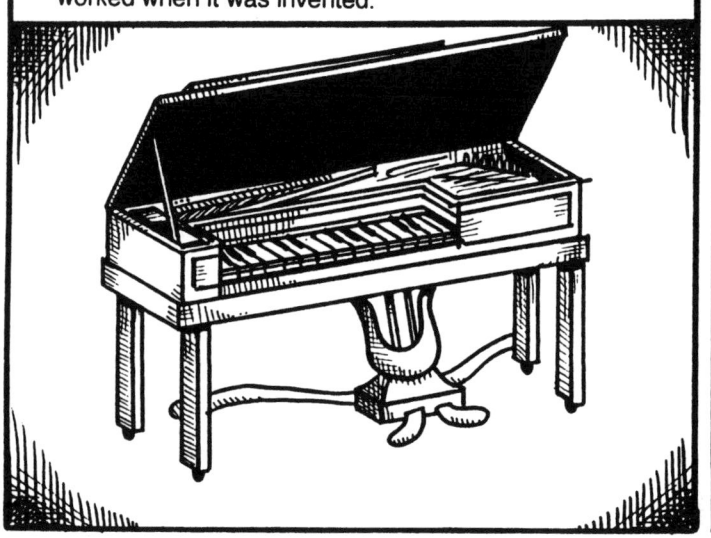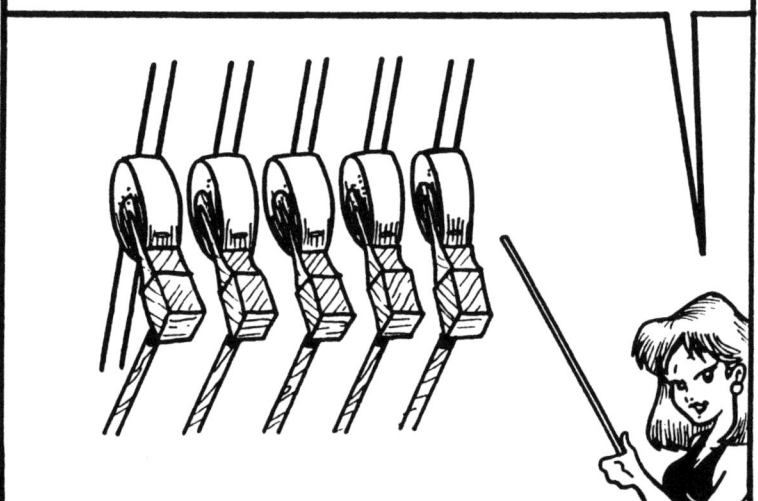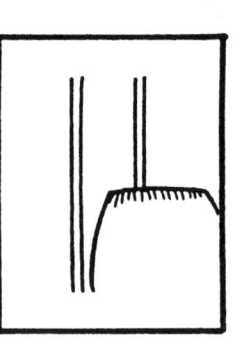

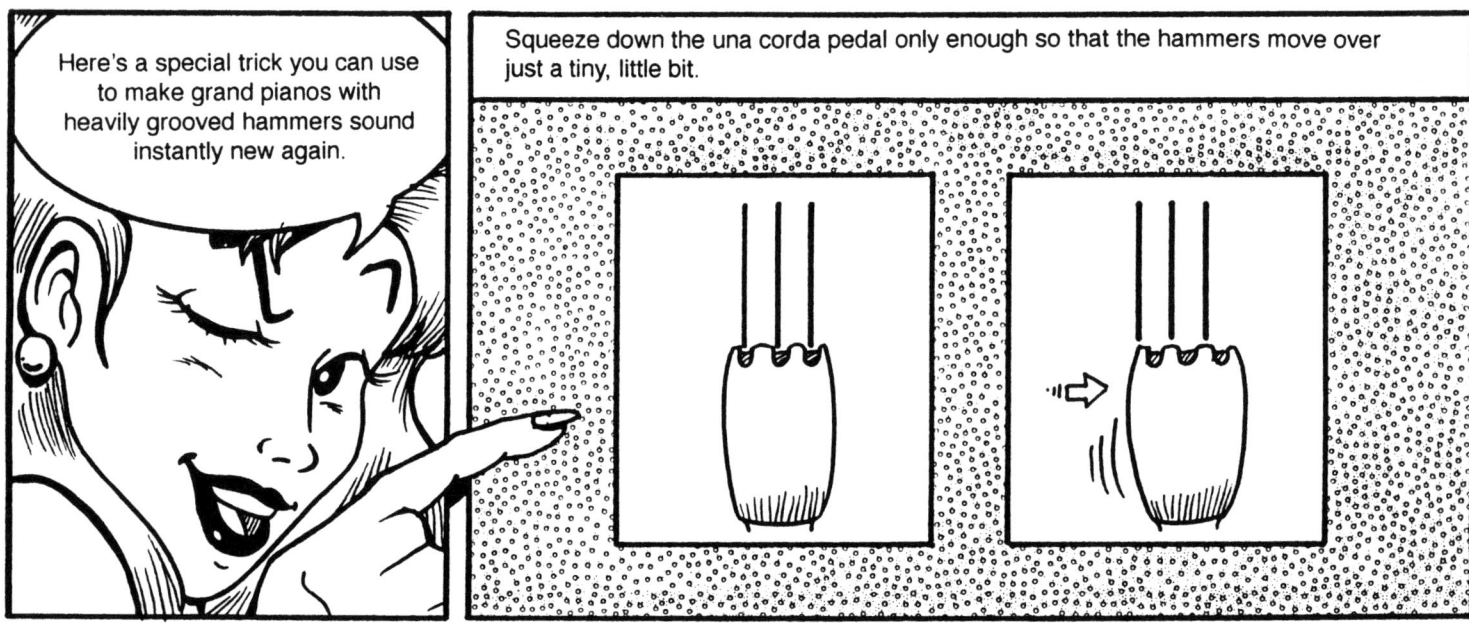

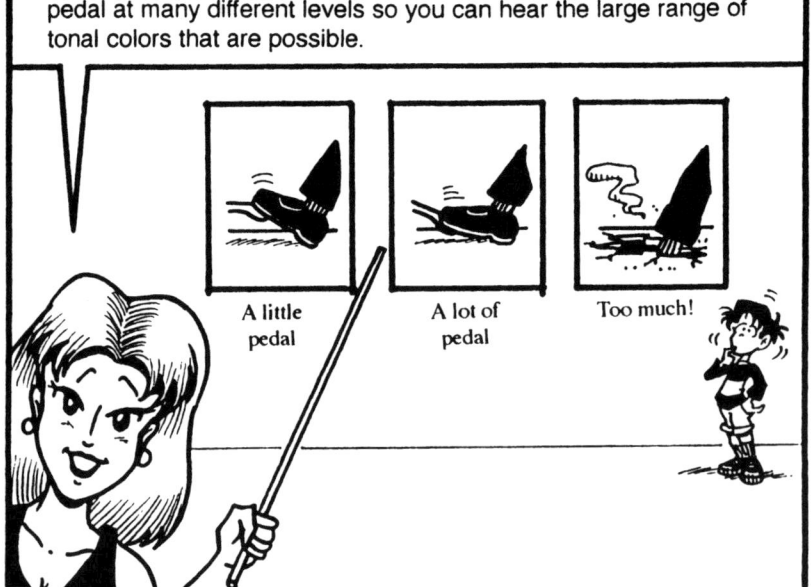

Some teachers worry that their students might use the pedal as a crutch for playing softly.

Other teachers enjoy the many tonal colors that the una corda pedal helps make and always recommend its use.

But all teachers agree that this pedal should never substitute for playing softly with the fingers when you want soft "singing" tones.

Composers or music editors usually write "u.c." or "una corda" when they want you to use the left pedal and "t.c." or "tre corde" when a return to the three strings is desired.

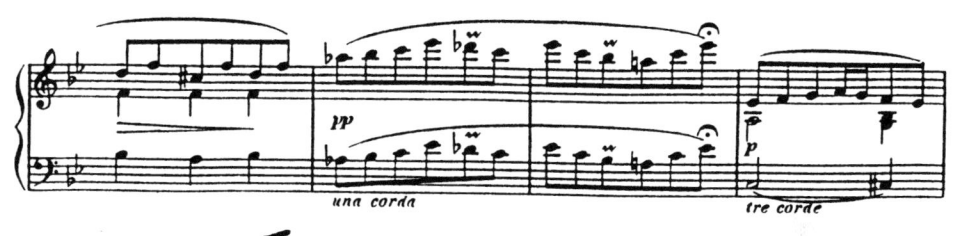

Albeniz *Songs of Spain, Op. 232, Prelude*

Composers sometimes use their own language to indicate una corda or a return to tre corde. You will often see instructions in French, "sourdine" and "3 cordes," or in Italian, "con sordino" (or "con sordina") and "senza sordini."

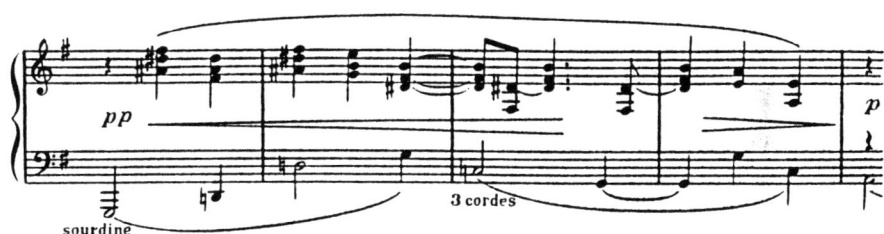

Ravel *Valse Nobles and Sentimentales, VIII Epilogue*

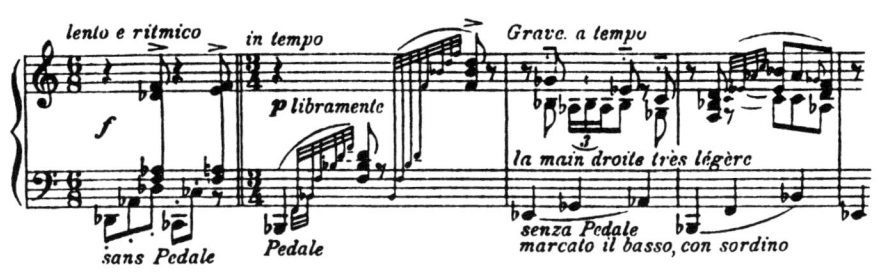

"sans" is French for "without"
"Pedale" is Italian for "damper pedal"
"senza Pedale" is Italian for "without pedal"
"Marcato il basso, con sordino" is Italian for "clearly stated bass with una corda pedal"

Granados *Goyescas, No. 2 Love Duet*

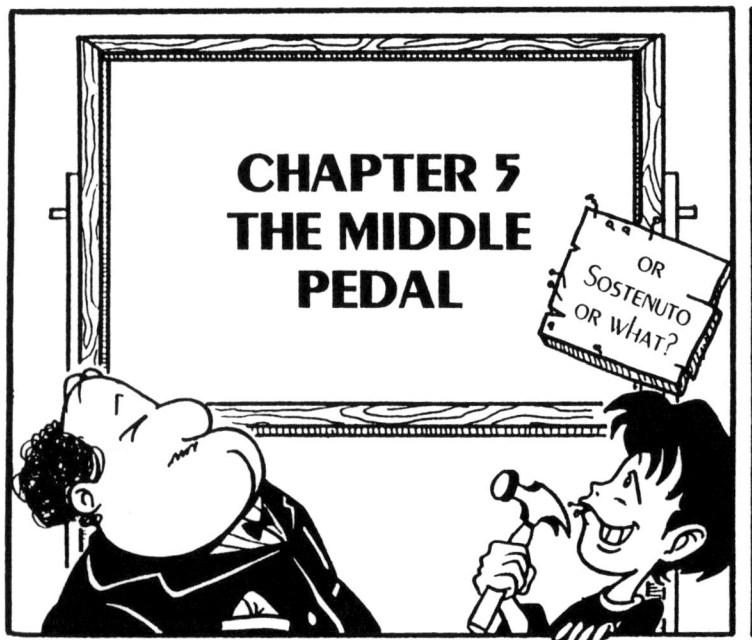

CHAPTER 5
THE MIDDLE PEDAL

OR SOSTENUTO OR WHAT?

THE SOSTENUTO PEDAL

The sostenuto pedal, usually the middle pedal on modern grand pianos, helps you sustain selected notes in one part of the keyboard while your hands are freed to play in another area.

To use it, first hold down the keys of the notes you wish to sustain with your fingers.

Next press down the middle pedal with your left foot and hold it down.

When your fingers come off the keys, the notes you were holding while you depressed the pedal will continue to sustain until you release the pedal.

The new notes you play as you are holding down the sostenuto pedal will not sustain unless you also use the damper pedal.

Musabella *Song for 13 Fingers, Op. 1*

(The way you learned to use it in chapters 1-3)

If you do use both pedals at the same time, be careful not to hold down the damper pedal as you depress the sostenuto pedal or many other notes will be sustained by mistake, causing a large, blurred sound.

The sostenuto pedal, invented in the nineteenth century, was used mostly in the United States until the middle of this century. Composers did not begin to call for its use until around 1950.

Europeans have not had much interest in this pedal. They began to add it to some of their pianos only after the second world war. Many fine European pianos are still made with only two pedals!

WHAT'S MISSING FROM THIS PICTURE?...

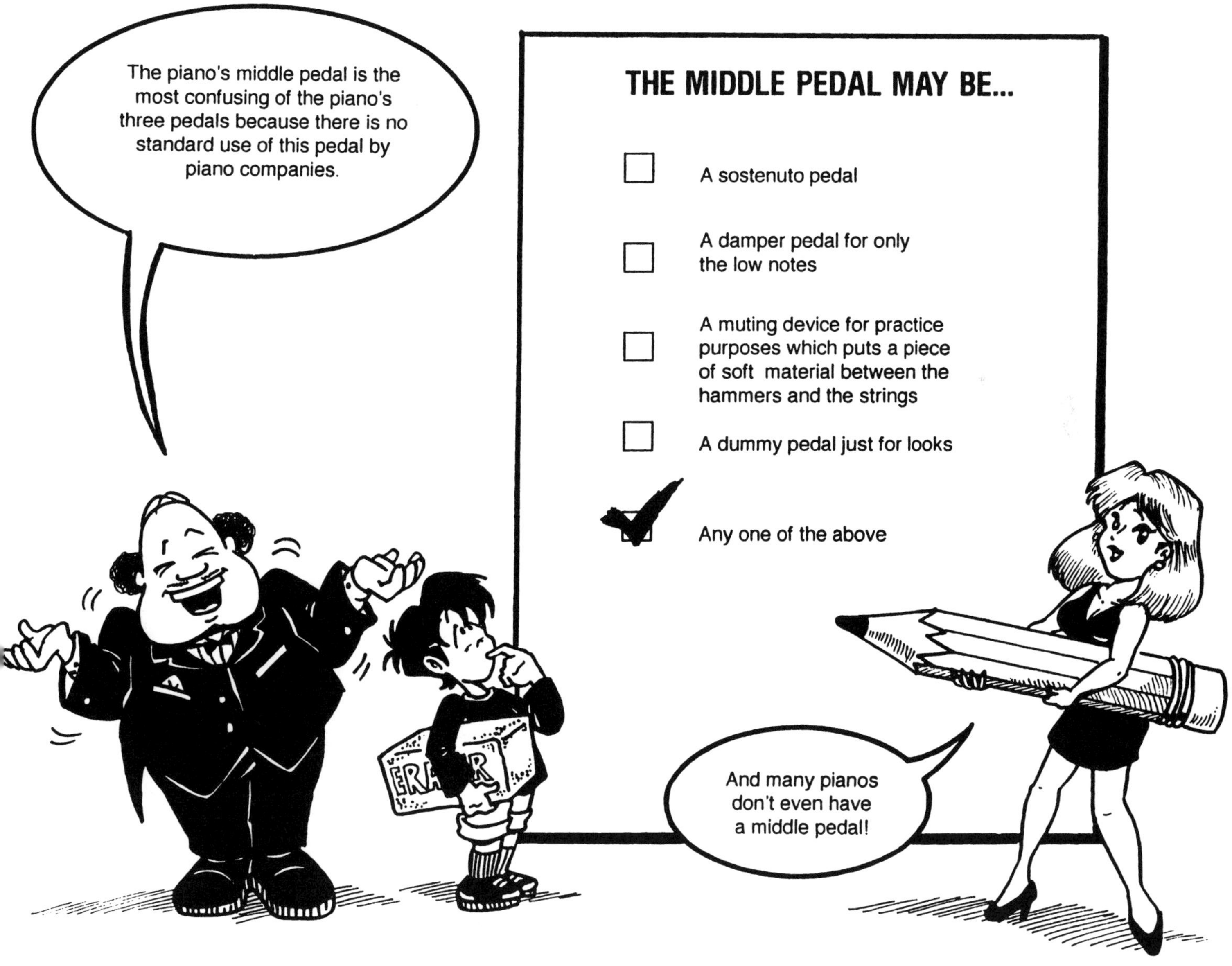

The piano's middle pedal is the most confusing of the piano's three pedals because there is no standard use of this pedal by piano companies.

THE MIDDLE PEDAL MAY BE...

☐ A sostenuto pedal

☐ A damper pedal for only the low notes

☐ A muting device for practice purposes which puts a piece of soft material between the hammers and the strings

☐ A dummy pedal just for looks

☑ Any one of the above

And many pianos don't even have a middle pedal!

Many pianists use the sostenuto pedal on the music of composers such as Debussy and Chopin, but most likely these composers never played on or even saw a piano that had a sostenuto pedal.

These composers probably intended you to create special musical textures with a variety of skillful damper pedal techniques such as sensitive half-damping or half-pedaling. (See Chapter 3)

When you play music of the past, it is necessary to adapt the pedaling to the instrument you are now playing. The sostenuto pedal is yet another tool for you to use to have additional control over the sound. (If you have skillful technique, use it tastefully along with all the other pedal techniques.) (Chapters 1 - 4)

If you plan to use this pedal in a performance, it would be wise to also practice without it in case this pedal does not work on the piano you will be playing.

WARNING!!!

Unfortunately, the sostenuto pedal is hardly ever found in perfect working condition. It is not very reliable.

Delicate lace is beautiful to us because of the spaces between the thin strands in the texture.

Space (silence) is just as important in a musical texture. As a general guideline, less pedal is usually better.

Music is language. It must have the right accents, inflections, and timing to have meaning. Books like this may help you understand how a language works, but you must hear native speakers speak the language, in numerous situations, to get the right "sound."

HI! THE BLUE GIRL ATE THE RED CAR YESTERDAY...

WHAT?!

Now that you know how the pedals work, the more you listen and study the pedaling of the great pianists, the faster you will develop your own fine pedaling technique.

A NOTE FROM THE AUTHOR

"PEDALING - THE SOUL OF THE PIANO"

The art of pedaling of pedaling is one of the most important of the numerous topics relating to the practice of piano performance. This humorous illustrated guide to the piano's pedals will enable pianists to understand and to begin using the pedals confidently from the start.

Although the first levers piano students learn to use are the piano's keys, the most misunderstood levers are the ones controlled by the feet - the pedals. Maestro Profondo, with the help of his assistant Musabella, introduces the piano's three pedals, (the damper, una corda, and sostenuto pedals) shows how they work, and includes numerous examples and suggestions for their effective use. He explores the pedal mechanism, explains fundamental foot placement and control, and surveys basic damper pedaling techniques such as syncopated, legato, treading, half-damper, and half-pedaling.

Profondo cannot and does not give absolute answers to the questions of the use of the pedal in individual interpretation because there are none. It is impossible to make absolute rules for when to pedal, what kind of pedal to use, or how much pedal to use. The art of pedaling relates to an awareness of historical style, the particular characteristics of the instrument being played, the performance venue, and especially to individual interpretation which is colored by the performer's personality.

Using the pedal correctly and artistically has to be cultivated and must never be automatic or random. Pedaling demands as much care as accurate playing with the correct articulation and expression. Sensitive pedaling requires the pianist to listen carefully to all sounds produced. It is an essential element in the production of beautiful piano sonorities and advanced piano performance.

Peter Coraggio

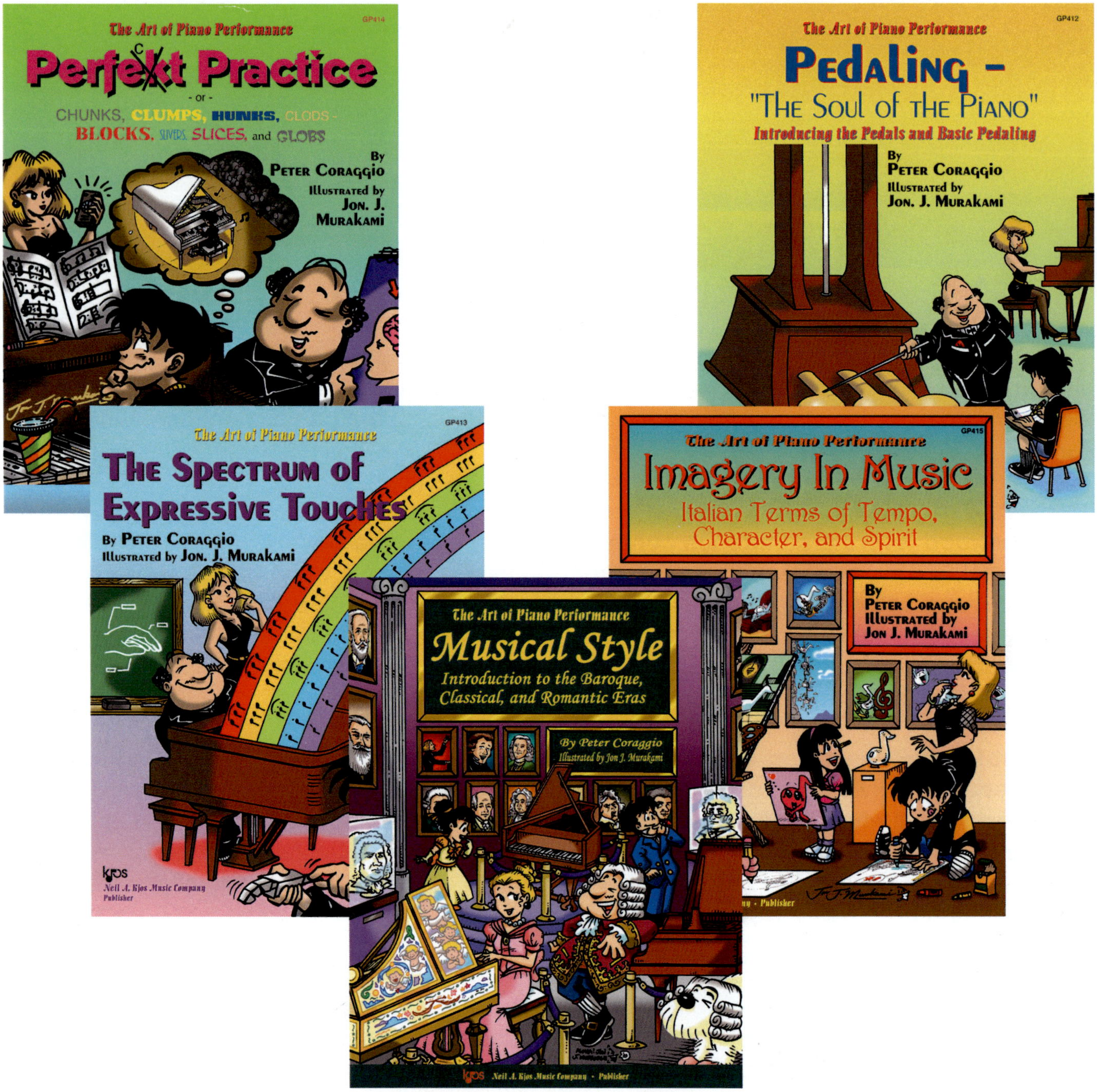

The Art of Piano Performance

By Peter Coraggio
Illustrated by Jon J. Murakami

Neil A. Kjos Music Company

ISBN: 0-8497-6215-4